This book is dedicated to all those Prince fans, "fams," true funk soldiers, bartenders, and mixologists throughout the world who seek the most authoritative, accurate, and complete source for perfect drinks inspired by beloved Prince songs.

"Shake Up Your Sexy"

lovesexy
cocktail guide

shake up your sexy

lovesexy
cocktail guide

andré akinyele
author & illustrator

ANDRÉ AKINYELE STUDIOS
SAN FRANCISCO   TORONTO

LoveSexy Cocktail Guide
First published in the United States in 2021 by

André Akinyele Studios
Toronto, Ontario M5V 3Z1 Canada
andreakinyelestudios@gmail.com
Visit www.andreakinyele.com

Text and design © André Akinyele 2021
Printed and bound in United States of America
10 9 8 7 6 5 4 3 2 1

Author's acknowledgements

My thanks to my family. Thanks to Prince Rogers Nelson, who served as an astonishing artist, entertainer, musician, and songwriter. He continues to inspire through the genius of his songwriting and song titles, a period of over 38 years, until his untimely death in 2016. My thanks also go to all the Prince fans, "Fams," True Funk Soldiers, and Purple Party People. Appreciation, as always, to the bartenders and mixologists around the world.

ISBN 978-1-66780-560-3

contents

sections

Welcome. You are holding in your hands the 1st Edition of the definitive guide to mixing perfect drinks inspired by Prince. The LoveSexy Cocktail Guide offers drinks inspired by beloved Prince songs and serves as an official manual for his fans, "fams," true funk soldiers, bartenders and mixologists. This cocktail book is a basic tool to prepare a Prince song inspired drink to "Get Yo Groove On" while listening to your favorite Prince song or drink inspired song. This book is urgently needed as a source on those days when you need a Prince "pick me up."

I've collected the best-known and best-loved Prince songs that could be inspired by drink recipes, tested and standardized by me, and presented in alphabetical order, with recipes clear and easy-to-follow that, at last, anyone could be an expert at Prince cocktail hour.

With all respect to Prince, this book is to honor him through his fans, "fams," true funk soldiers, and purple party people that drink spirits or like having cocktails every now and then.

The LoveSexy Cocktail Guide is not stuffy or complicated, and contains recipes for spirits, mixers, and ingredients that an alcoholic, I mean drunk... no sorry...I mean any person who drinks spirits and cocktails might already have on hand.

introduction

These drinks are meant to celebrate Prince through inspired song, good times, and good friends who also love Prince and his music. You will make memorable drinks for your Prince inspired parties and a perfect excuse to put on his music and get lost in "spirits," song, and dance.

Okay, as Prince once said,

"Shut up already, damn!"

Now, turn the page and let's get started!!!

ingredients you should have on hand

Alcoholic Beverages

Brandy
Coffee Liqueur
Gin
Rum (Light and Dark)
Scotch
Tequila
Triple Sec
Vermouth (Dry and Sweet)
Vodka
Whiskey

Non-Alcoholic Mixers

Carbonated Water
Cream
Eggs
Ginger Ale
Grape Juice
Grapefruit Juice
Lemon Juice
Lime Juice
Maple Syrup
Milk
Orange Juice
Pineapple Juice
Sugar Syrup

Garnishing's

Bitters (Angostura, Ginger, Lime, Orange)
Cayenne Pepper
Food Coloring
Lemons
Limes
Maraschino Cherries / Juice
Mint Leaves / Sprigs
Olives (Black and Green)
Onions (White)
Oranges
Pineapple (Slices, Strips, or Rings)
Powdered Sugar
Raspberries (Fresh or Frozen)
Salt (Coarse)
Sugar (Brown and White)
Sugar Lumps
Swizzle Sticks

a...alphabet street

Anna Stesia is the fourth track on Prince's tenth album Lovesexy released
May 10, 1988.

anna stesia
album: lovesexy

1½ oz.	Gin
1 dash	Orange Bitters
¼	Orange Juiced

Serves 1

1. Shake with ice and strain into cocktail glass.

Annie Christian is the seventh track on Prince's fourth album Controversy released October 14, 1981. The song's lyrics mention the killing of singer-songwriter John Lennon by Mark David Chapman on December 8, 1980 in New York City; the assassination attempt of Ronald Reagan on March 30, 1981; the Atlanta, GA murders that took place between the summer of 1979 and the spring of 1981 where a series of murders on afro-American children adolescents and young adults were committed; that several of the victims were last seen getting into a blue car; and Abscam, an FBI sting operation in the late 1970s and early 1980s that initially targeted trafficking in stolen property but later converted to a public corruption investigation.

annie christian
album: controversy

1½ oz.	Vodka
1 dash	Triple Sec
1 tbsp.	Pineapple Juice
¼	Lemon Juiced
1	Lemon Wedge

Serves 1

1. Shake with ice and strain into cocktail glass.

2. Garnish with lemon wedge.

Another Lonely Christmas is the seventeenth track on disc three:
The B-Sides of Prince's compilation album The Hits / The B-Sides
released September 14, 1993, and was the b-side of I Would Die 4 U
released November 28, 1984 the fourth single from the album Purple
Rain. The track is the only Christmas-related song Prince has released.

another lonely christmas
album: the hits / the b-sides

1½ oz.	Gin
¾ oz.	Sweet Vermouth

Serves 1

1. Stir with ice and strain into cocktail glass.

Anotherloverholenyohead is the eleventh track on Prince's eighth album Parade (Prince and the Revolution) released March 31, 1986, and is the album's third single released July 2, 1986.

anotherloverholenyohead
album: parade

1¾ oz.	Scotch
¾ oz.	Dry Vermouth
1 dash	Orange Bitters
¼ tsp.	Lemon Juice

Serves 1

1. Shake with ice and strain into cocktail glass.

Arboretum is the tenth track on Prince's twenty-fifth album One Nite Alone.... released May 14, 2002, and was recorded in the atrium of Paisley Park Studios. Prince credited his pet doves Divinity and Majesty as providing ambient singing on the track, as their cage was in the upstairs hallway overlooking the atrium.

arboretum
album: one nite alone... (solo piano & voice)

1½ oz.	Rum (Dark)
1 oz.	Coffee Liqueur
1	Egg White
	Cracked Ice

Serves 1

1. Shake all ingredients with cracked ice and strain into cocktail glass.

Automatic is the sixth track on Prince's fifth album 1999 released October 27, 1982.

automatic
album: 1999

1 oz.	Scotch
1 oz.	Dry Vermouth
1 oz.	Sweet Vermouth
3 dashes	Orange Bitters

Serves 1

1. Stir with ice and strain into cocktail glass.

Avalanche is the seventh track on Prince's twenty-fifth album One Nite Alone.... released May 14, 2002.

avalanche
album: one nite alone... (solo piano & voice)

1½ oz.	Gin
1½ tsp.	Sweet Vermouth
2 dashes	Angostura Bitters

Serves 1

1. Stir with ice and strain into cocktail glass.

b...beautiful strange

Baby I'm A Star is the eighth track on Prince's sixth album Purple Rain (Prince and the Revolution) released June 25, 1984, and was the b-side of Take Me With U the album's fifth single released January 25, 1985. In 1989, Tim Burton used the track in a rough draft of the Batman movie, during a scene where The Joker leads a parade of large balloons, to indicate the kind of music he wanted in that scene. Prince provided 200 Balloons as a replacement, which was eventually replaced by the song Trust.

baby i'm a star
album: purple rain

2 oz.	Brandy
2 dashes	Angostura Bitters
¼ tsp.	Sugar Syrup
	Lemon Peel Twist

Serves 1

1. In saucepan, stir 1¼ cups sugar into ¾ cups hot water to make 1 cup of simple syrup.

2. Stir all ingredients with ice and strain into cocktail glass.

3. Garnish with lemon peel twist.

Bambi is the sixth track on Prince's second album, self-titled,
Prince released October 19, 1979, and was the b-side of Still Waiting
the album's third single released March 25, 1980.

bambi
album: prince

1½ oz.	Gin
½ oz.	Dry Vermouth
½ tsp.	Sweet Vermouth
1½ tsp.	Triple Sec
	Lemon Peel Twist

Serves 1

1. Stir with ice and strain into cocktail glass.

2. Garnish with lemon peel twist.

Beautiful Strange is the eleventh track on Prince's remix album
Rave In2 The Joy Fantastic released April 30, 2001 and the companion
album to Prince's 23rd album Rave Un2 The Joy Fantastic released
November 9, 1999. The song was the only track on the album not to
have been included on Rave Un2 The Joy Fantastic, and was first
available as a video of a studio recording ending the Beautiful Strange
home video released August 24, 1999 with a short segment of the
recording session included as a prologue to the home video.

beautiful strange
album: rave in2 the joy fantastic

½ oz.	Brandy
½ oz.	Light Rum
½ oz.	Triple Sec
¼	Lemon Juiced

Serves 1

1. Shake with ice and strain into cocktail glass.

Beautiful, Loved and Blessed (a.k.a. Beautiful, Loved & Blessed) is the tenth track on Prince's thirty-first album 3121 released March 21, 2006, and was the b-side of Black Sweat the album's first single released March 27, 2006 with a slightly different ending.

beautiful, loved, & blessed
album: 3121

¾ oz.	Gin
¾ oz.	Light Rum
¾ oz.	Dry Vermouth

Serves 1

1. Stir with ice and strain into cocktail glass.

Big City is the twelfth track on Prince's thirty-ninth and final album HitnRun Phase Two released December 12, 2015, and first streamed as a live rehearsal on 3rdEye TV Show #4 on June 23, 2013.

big city
album: hitnrun phase two

1 oz.	Dry Vermouth
1 oz.	Sweet Vermouth
1 dash	Angostura Bitters
1 dash	Orange Bitters
	Orange Peel Twist
	Cracked Ice

Serves 1

1. Stir with cracked ice and strain into cocktail glass.

2. Garnish with orange peel twist.

Billy Jack Bitch is the fifteenth track on Prince's seventeenth album The Gold Experience released September 26, 1995. The track's chorus features background vocals by Lenny Kravitz, who was not credited as he was on a different record label. The track marks as their only known studio collaboration to have been released. The track is retaliation against Minneapolis gossip columnist C.J. (Cheryl Johnson), who regularly wrote negative articles about Prince.

billy jack bitch
album: the gold experience

1½ oz.	Gin
2 dashes	Orange Bitters
½	Lime Juiced
½ tsp.	Powdered Sugar

Serves 1

1. Shake with ice and strain into cocktail glass.

Black Muse is the tenth track on Prince's thirty-ninth and final album HitnRun Phase Two released December 12, 2015. The last 3 minutes and 5 seconds of the track contains the song 1000 Light Years From Here, ultimately released July 30, 2021 as the fourth track of his posthumous album Welcome 2 America.

black muse
album: hitnrun phase two

| 1½ oz. | Vodka |
| 3⁄4 oz. | Coffee Liqueur |

Serves 1

1. Pour over ice cubes in cocktail glass.

Black Sweat is the fourth track on Prince's thirty-first album 3121 released March 21, 2006, and was released as a download as the album's second single released February 21, 2006. Prince added the track to the acoustic section of the Musicology Live 2004ever tour on June 25, 2004. The live recording of Black Sweat from Prince's final full show from April 14, 2016 at the Fox Theatre, Atlanta, GA, was made available on Tidal on April 18, 2016 as the Purple Pick of the Week, and became the final official release of music by Prince before his death on April 21, 2016.

black sweat
album: 3121

2 oz.	Light Rum
½ oz.	Dry Vermouth
	Black Food Coloring (Optional)
	Black Olive
	Cracked Ice

Serves 1

1. Stir with cracked ice and strain into cocktail glass.

2. Stir in food coloring (optional) – Mix equal amounts of red, blue, and yellow together to get a nice black color.

3. Garnish with black olive.

Blue Light is the seventh track on Prince's fourteenth album 🜍
(Prince and the New Power Generation) released October 13, 1992.

blue light
album: love symbol

1½ oz.	Vodka
¾ oz.	Triple Sec
1 dash	Blue Food Coloring

Serves 1

1. Stir with ice and strain into cocktail glass.

Bob George is the fifth track on Prince's sixteenth album The Black Album officially released November 22, 1994. But, the album was widely bootlegged after its initial cancellation in 1987. A live version of the track was included on the Lovesexy Live 2 VHS home video released April 19, 1989, taken from the September 9, 1988 live TV broadcast. As Prince performed the track on the Lovesexy Tour, at the end of the song the character "Bob George" (Prince played) was shot. Prince allowed Madonna to sample the track years before its official release. The line "skinny motherfucker with a high voice" was sampled on a remix for her Like A Prayer (released on a promo edition of the single in 1989).

bob george
album: the black album

1¼ oz.	Whiskey
1½ oz.	Gin

Serves 1

1. Stir with ice and strain into cocktail glass.

Boom is the second track on Prince's thirty-third album Lotusflow3r released March 24, 2009.

boom
album: lotusflow3r

¾ oz.	Brandy
¾ oz.	Light Rum
¾ oz.	Triple Sec
½	Lime Juiced

Serves 1

1. Shake with ice and strain into cocktail glass.

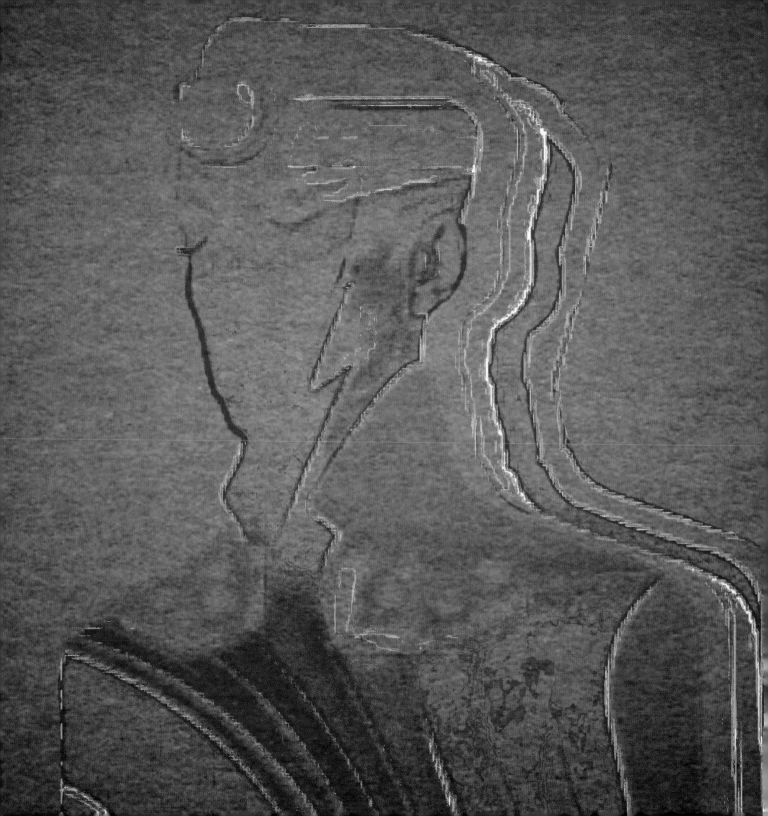

c...colonized mind

Calhoun Square is the third track on the second disc of Prince's twentieth album Crystal Ball released January 29, 1998, and named after the Calhoun Square shopping mall (located in the Uptown district of Minneapolis, Minnesota). Until October 2020, the building was previously known as Calhoun Square but now Seven Points.

calhoun square
album: crystal ball

1 oz.	Gin
½ oz.	Dry Vermouth
½ oz.	Sweet Vermouth
	Mint Sprig

Serves 1

1. Shake with ice and strain into cocktail glass.

2. Garnish with mint sprig.

Chaos and Disorder is the first track on Prince's eighteenth album Chaos and Disorder released July 9, 1996.

chaos and disorder
album: chaos and disorder

1½ oz.	Whiskey
2 dashes	Orange Bitters
½	Lime Juiced
1 tsp.	Powdered Sugar

Serves 1

1. Shake with ice and strain into cocktail glass.

Chelsea Rodgers is the eighth track from Prince's thirty-second album Planet Earth released July 15, 2007, and inspired by and written about model and clothing designer Chelsea Rodgers.

chelsea rodgers
album: planet earth

¾ oz.	Gin
¾ oz.	Triple Sec
¼	Lemon Juiced

Serves 1

1. Shake with ice and strain into cocktail glass.

Christopher Tracy's Parade (a.k.a. Wendy's Parade) is the first track on Prince's eighth album Parade (Prince and the Revolution) released March 31, 1986. The track is named after his character (Christopher Tracy) in his second feature film Under The Cherry Moon. Initially, the track was named after Revolution guitarist Wendy Melvoin.

christopher tracy's parade
album: parade

1½ oz.	Brandy
1½ oz.	Sweet Vermouth
1 dash	Angostura Bitters

Serves 1

1. Shake with ice and strain into cocktail glass.

Cindy C. is the second track on Prince's sixteenth album The Black Album released November 22, 1994. But, the album was widely bootlegged after its initial cancellation in 1987. The track's title refers to supermodel Cindy Crawford. Prince was unaware that Cat's rap in the track was taken from J.M. Silk's 1985 song Music Is The Key. The rap was later reused in an unreleased version of Positivity, but Prince removed it after finding out about its origins.

cindy c.
album: the black album

| 1½ oz. | Brandy |
| ¾ oz. | Sweet Vermouth |

Serves 1

1. Stir with ice and strain into cocktail glass.

Colonized Mind is the fifth track on Prince's thirty-third album Lotusflow3r released March 24, 2009, and premiered on the Los Angeles radio station Indie 103 on December 18, 2008.

colonized mind
album: lotusflow3r

1½ oz.	Gin
¾ oz.	Sweet Vermouth
	Olive

Serves 1

1. Stir with ice and strain into cocktail glass.

2. Garnish with olive.

Compassion is the first track from Prince's thirty-fifth album 20Ten released July 10, 2010.

compassion
album: 20ten

¾ oz.	Light Rum
1½ oz.	Pineapple Juice
½ tsp.	Lemon Juice

Serves 1

1. Shake with ice and strain into cocktail glass.

Condition Of The Heart is the third track on Prince's seventh album Around The World In A Day (Prince and the Revolution) released April 22, 1985. The lyrics refer to Clara Bow, an American film actress who rose to fame during the 1920s, and her image is featured on the front cover of the album's artwork.

condition of the heart
album: around the world in a day

2 oz.	Light Rum
½	Lime Juiced
½ tsp.	Powdered Sugar

Serves 1

1. Shake with ice and strain into cocktail glass.

Cream is the fourth track on Prince's thirteenth album Diamonds and Pearls (Prince and the New Power Generation) released October 1, 1991, and was the album's second single released September 9, 1991.

cream
album: diamonds and pearls

1½ oz.	Whiskey
1 tbsp.	Cream

Serves 1

1. Shake with ice and strain into cocktail glass.

Crystal Ball is the first track on the first disc of Prince's twentieth album Crystal Ball released January 29, 1998.

crystal ball
album: crystal ball

1½ oz.	Gin
1½ oz.	Dry Vermouth
½	Lime Juiced

Serves 1

1. Shake with ice and strain into cocktail glass.

Curious Child is the fifth track on the second disc of Prince's nineteenth album Emancipation released November 19, 1996.

curious child
album: emancipation

1oz.	Light Rum
½ tsp.	Triple Sec
1 tbsp.	Pineapple Juice
½	Lime Juiced
	Pineapple Slice

Serves 1

1. Shake with ice and strain into cocktail glass.

2. Garnish with pineapple slice.

d...darling nikki

77

D.M.S.R. (a.k.a Dance Music Sex Romance) is the fifth track on Prince's fifth album 1999 released October 27, 1982. An edit of the track was included as the eighth track on the Risky Business movie soundtrack released in 1984, and was included in the movie starring Tom Cruise.

d.m.s.r
album: 1999

1½ oz.	Gin
1½ tsp.	Dry Vermouth
1½ tsp.	Sweet Vermouth
	Orange Peel Twist

Serves 1

1. Stir with ice and strain into cocktail glass.

2. Garnish with orange peel twist.

Daddy Pop is the second track on Prince's thirteenth album Diamonds and Pearls (Prince and the New Power Generation) released October 1, 1991, and was included on some versions of the Sexy MF single in 1992. To create the songs ending, the song was edited together with the ending of a rehearsal performance of Partyman. The track includes a sampled drum loop from Aretha Franklin's song Rock Steady from her 1972 album Young, Gifted and Black.

daddy pop
album: diamonds and pearls

1½ oz.	Gin
½ oz.	Dry Vermouth
	Lemon Peel Twist
	Olive

Serves 1

1. Stir vermouth and gin over ice cubes.

2. Strain into cocktail glass.

3. Garnish with lemon peel twist and olive.

Damn U is the eleventh track on Prince's fourteenth album ⚥
(Prince and the New Power Generation) released October 13, 1992,
and was the album's fourth single released November 17, 1992.

damn u
album: love symbol

1 oz.	Gin
1 tbsp.	Sweet Vermouth
1 tsp.	Triple Sec
1 tbsp.	Orange Juice

Serves 1

1. Shake with ice and strain into cocktail glass.

Darling Nikki is the fifth track on Prince's sixth album Purple Rain (Prince and the Revolution) released June 25, 1984. Notes from Prince's Dreams notebook that was on display at the "My Name Is Prince" exhibit in the O2 in London revealed that Prince considered naming Vanity's character in the film Nicarthra Ann, Nikki for short (ultimately changed to Apollonia). Tipper Gore (wife of Al Gore), having overheard her eleven-year-old daughter listening to the track, was inspired to found the Parents Music Resource Center that advocated the mandatory use of the warning label "Parental Advisory: Explicit Lyrics" on record covers "thought" to contain language or lyrical content unsuitable for minors. The recording industry voluntarily complied with the Center's request.

darling nikki
album: purple rain

2 oz.	Vodka
1 oz.	Light Rum
½ oz.	Milk
½	Lemon Juiced
1 tsp.	Sugar
	Lemon Peel Twist

Serves 1

1. Shake with ice and strain into cocktail glass.

2. Garnish with lemon peel twist.

Days Of Wild is the first track on the third disc of Prince's twentieth album Crystal Ball released January 29, 1998, and is a live version recorded December 9, 1995 at Paisley Park Studios in Chanhassen, Minnesota. The track's lead line is a modified version of the lead line from Caravan, a jazz standard composed by Juan Tizol and first performed by Duke Ellington in 1936. The track contains repeated vocal samples of "Hold on to your wigs" and "Diss me" from Ninety-9's tracks The Mood For Love and Burns 1 (both containing input by Prince). The sampled strings in the opening of the Crystal Ball version are sampled from Violet The Organ Grinder.

days of wild
album: crystal ball

1½ oz.	Light Rum
1	Lime Juiced
1 tsp.	Powdered Sugar

Serves 1

1. Shake with ice and strain into cocktail glass.

Delirious is the third track on Prince's fifth album 1999 released October 27, 1982, and was the third single released August 17, 1983 from the album 1999. A full length version of the track was released November 29, 2019 as the second track on Disc 4: Vault Tracks 2 of the 1999 (Super Deluxe) Edition.

delirious
album: 1999

1½ oz.	Gin
1 oz.	Dry Vermouth
1 dash	Orange Bitters
	Lemon Peel Twist

Serves 1

1. Stir with ice and strain into cocktail glass.

2. Garnish with lemon peel twist.

Digital Garden is the third track on Prince's twenty-fourth album
The Rainbow Children released November 20, 2001, his first album
after reverting back to the name Prince. Initially, the album was released
October 16, 2001 as an NPG Music Club download. The track was
included as the fourth track on the She Loves Me 4 Me "Jazz Sampler"
promo CD released late 2001.

digital garden
album: the rainbow children

2 oz.	Gin
½ oz.	Triple Sec
1 tbsp.	Pineapple Juice

Serves 1

1. Shake with ice and strain into cocktail glass.

Dionne is the fifth track on Prince's twenty-first album The Truth released January 29, 1998. In 1999 during a Love4oneanother.com "? of the week," a fan (using the name Dionne) asked about the inspiration for the song, to which Prince replied: "Dionne lives in London and knows quite well the heart she broke. All Dionnes r heartbreakers!" Since singer Dionne Farris was sent a tape with the song, she stated that the line "Did u get the tape eye sent u, Eye thought it be better in a song" (from the tenth track One Of Your Tears from the same album) refers to this happening.

dionne
album: the truth

1½ oz.	Whiskey
¼	Lemon Juiced
½ tsp.	Powdered Sugar
	Mint Leaf

Serves 1

1. Shake with ice and strain into cocktail glass.

2. Garnish with mint leaf.

Dirty Mind is the first track on Prince's third album Dirty Mind released October 8, 1980, and was the album's second single released November 26, 1980. The song is the first time a band member (Dr. Fink) was given co-writing credit for music, as he had developed the repeated synth line. Prince's keyboardist Matt Fink "became known as" Dr. Fink while playing the opening act with Prince during the early stages of the Rick James Tour '80, when he replaced a jailbird costume with a surgical costume to avoid comparisons with Rick James who was also performing in a jailbird costume during the same tour.

dirty mind
album: dirty mind

½ oz.	Brandy
¾ oz.	Gin
½ oz.	Dry Vermouth
½ oz.	Sweet Vermouth
	Lemon Peel Twist

Serves 1

1. Stir with ice and strain into cocktail glass.

2. Garnish with lemon peel twist.

Dolphin is the eighth track on Prince's seventeenth album The Gold Experience released September 26, 1995. A promo video for the track was premiered as the first video to be broadcast on VH-1 Europe on September 30, 1994. Prince performed the track live on The Late Show with David Letterman at The Ed Sullivan Theater in New York City on December 13, 1994. In early 1995, a rehearsal version was included on Prince's The Undertaker VHS released March 6, 1995. The track was available as a promotional cassette single released in late summer 1995.

dolphin
album: the gold experience

1½ oz.	Gin
½ oz.	Triple Sec
1 dash	Angostura Bitters
¼	Lemon Juiced

Serves 1

1. Shake with ice and strain into cocktail glass.

Dreamer is the eleventh track on Prince's thirty-third album Lotusflow3r released March 24, 2009. The track was said to be inspired by African-American comedian, social activist, social critic, writer and entrepreneur Dick Gregory. In March 2009, a 30-second Target commercial for the album featured Prince performing a segment of Dreamer. On December 2, 2009, Dreamer was nominated for a Grammy for "Best Solo Rock Vocal Performance;" the first time a Prince song had been nominated for a Grammy without being released as a promo or commercial single. On January 31, 2010, in a pre-show ceremony, Dreamer lost the Grammy to Bruce Springsteen's Working On A Dream. Prince performed the track live on The Tonight Show with Jay Leno in Burbank, CA March 26, 2009.

dreamer
album: lotusflow3r

1½ oz.	Gin
¾ oz.	Sweet Vermouth
	Orange Slice

Serves 1

1. Stir with ice and strain into cocktail glass.

2. Garnish with orange slice.

e...erotic city

Electric Chair is the second track on Prince's eleventh album Batman released June 20, 1989. A remix of the track by William Orbit was the b-side of The Future released May 18, 1990 the album's fifth single. The vocals are attributed to The Joker, a character from the movie, as if Prince is singing on his behalf.

electric chair
album: batman

1½ oz.	Gin
¾ oz.	Dry Vermouth
¼ tsp.	Sweet Vermouth
	Lemon Peel Twist

Serves 1

1. Stir with ice and strain into cocktail glass.

2. Garnish with lemon peel twist.

Emancipation is the twelfth track on the third disc of Prince's nineteenth album Emancipation released November 19, 1996.

emancipation
album: emancipation

1 oz.	Gin
½ oz.	Dry Vermouth
½ oz.	Sweet Vermouth
2 dashes	Angostura Bitters

Serves 1

1. Stir with ice and strain into cocktail glass.

Erotic City (a.k.a. Erotic City ("Make Love Not War Erotic City Come Alive") is the ninth track on disc three: The B-Sides of Prince's The Hits / The B-Sides compilation album released September 14, 1993, and was the b-side of Let's Go Crazy released July 18, 1984 the second single from the album Purple Rain. Although credited to Prince and the Revolution, only Prince and Sheila E. contributed to the track. The song is notable as the first Prince release to contain input from Sheila E., although her album The Glamorous Life was mostly written, performed and produced by Prince.

erotic city
album: the hits / b-sides

1½ oz.	Light Rum
¾ oz.	Dry Vermouth
1 dash	Angostura Bitters

Serves 1

1. Stir with ice and strain into cocktail glass.

f...for you

109

Face Down is the fourth track on the third disc of Prince's nineteenth album Emancipation released November 19, 1996, and uses the sampled phrase "Dead like Elvis" by Ninety-9's song Stained Glass. A live version of the track was included on a cassette on NYC (a cassette single sold for $20.00 directly from the 1-800 New Funk phone service) released January 31, 1997.

face down
album: emancipation

2 oz.	Brandy
¼ tsp.	Triple Sec
1 dash	Angostura Bitters
¼ tsp.	Powdered Sugar
	Lemon Peel Twist

Serves 1

1. Shake with ice and strain into cocktail glass.

2. Garnish with lemon peel twist.

Fascination is the ninth track on Prince's twenty-first album The Truth released January 29, 1998.

fascination
album: the truth

1 oz.	Scotch
1 oz.	Sweet Vermouth
1 dash	Angostura Bitters
¼ tsp.	Sugar Syrup

Serves 1

1. In saucepan, stir 1¼ cups sugar into ¾ cups hot water to make 1 cup of simple syrup.

2. Stir all ingredients with ice and strain into cocktail glass.

Funknroll is the twelfth track on Prince's thirty-sixth album Plectrumelectrum (Prince and 3rdEyeGirl) released September 30, 2014, and the eleventh track on his thirty-seventh album Art Official Age as a remix also released September 30, 2014. Prince and 3rdEyeGirl performed the track on The Arsenio Hall Show March 4, 2014.

funknroll
album: art official age / plectrumelectrum

1½ oz.	Gin
½ oz.	Dry Vermouth
1 dash	Sweet Vermouth
1 dash	Triple Sec

Serves 1

1. Shake with ice and strain into cocktail glass.

Fury is the eighth track on Prince's thirty-first album 3121 released March 21, 2006.

fury
album: 3121

2 oz.	Whiskey
¼ tsp.	Triple Sec
1 dash	Angostura Bitters
¼ tsp.	Powdered Sugar
	Lemon Peel Twist

Serves 1

1. Shake with ice and strain into cocktail glass.

2. Garnish with lemon peel twist.

Future Baby Mama is the fifth track from Prince's thirty-second album Planet Earth released July 15, 2007, and was the album's third single. The track won the Grammy Award for "Best Male R&B Vocal Performance" on February 10, 2008.

future baby mama
album: planet earth

1½ oz.	Light Rum
¾ oz.	Sweet Vermouth
½ tsp.	Triple Sec

Serves 1

1. Stir with ice and strain into cocktail glass.

g...get yo groove on

121

Gamillah is the ninth track on Prince's twenty-ninth album The Chocolate Invasion released March 29, 2004, and was the b-side of The Daisy Chain (The New Power Generation) single released April 14, 2001 sold only at concerts on Prince's Hit N Run Tour. The track was included as a download part of NPG Music Club Edition #11 but credited to Prince. The song features Najee, who plays soprano saxophone on the track.

gamillah
album: the chocolate invasion

1½ oz.	Gin
1 oz.	Lime Juice
1 tsp.	Powdered Sugar

Serves 1

1. Shake with ice and strain into cocktail glass.

Gett Off is the seventh track on Prince's thirteenth album Diamonds and Pearls (Prince and the New Power Generation) released October 1, 1991, and was the album's first single released July 29, 1991. The track was initially released to DJs as a promo on Prince's 33rd birthday, June 7, 1991. The track was the earliest song to be released with credit to Prince and the New Power Generation. The song borrows from Get Off (with one "t"), released in 1990 on the New Power Generation maxi-single, and was developed with portions of a song called Glam Slam '91. Prince performed the track live at the 1991 MTV Music Awards September 5, 1991. Various versions of this song include both a sample and reference to James Brown's Mother Popcorn.

gett off
album: diamonds and pearls

1½ oz.	Gin
¾ oz.	Dry Vermouth
2 dashes	Angostura Bitters

Serves 1

1. Stir with ice and strain into cocktail glass.

Girls & Boys is the fifth track on Prince's eighth album Parade
(Prince and the Revolution) released March 31, 1986, and was the
b-side of Anotherloverholenyohead the album's third single released
July 2, 1986. The spoken French word on the original recording (referred
to as "French seduction" on liner notes) is credited to costume designer
Marie France.

girls & boys
album: parade

| | Gin |
| ½ tsp. | Angostura Bitters |

Serves 1

1. In a cocktail glass put bitters.

2. Revolve glass until it is entirely coated with the bitters.

3. Fill with gin, no ice.

Glam Slam is the third track on Prince's tenth album Lovesexy released May 10, 1988, and was the second single released July 11, 1988. Prince decided a few days before the single's release that it was the wrong choice for a second single and tried to stop its release. The term Glam Slam was the name of his nightclubs in Minneapolis, Tokyo, Miami Beach and Los Angeles in the early 1990s. Prince later used the term for the 'VIP' virtual nightclub on the NPG Music Club, where dance tracks by Prince were streamed during weekends in May 2003.

glam slam
album: lovesexy

2 oz.	Gin
2 dashes	Angostura Bitters
2 oz.	Carbonated Water
1	Lime Juiced
1 tsp.	Powdered Sugar
	Swizzle Stick

Serves 1

1. In a cocktail glass put lime juice, powdered sugar, and carbonated water.

2. Fill glass with ice and stir.

3. Add bitters and gin, and fill with carbonated water.

4. Serve with swizzle stick.

Gold is the eighteenth track on Prince's seventeenth album The Gold Experience released September 26, 1995, and was the album's second single released November 30, 1995.

gold
album: the gold experience

1½ oz.	Gin
1½ oz.	Triple Sec
1 dash	Orange Bitters
1 tbsp.	Pineapple Juice

Serves 1

1. Shake with ice and strain into cocktail glass.

Golden Parachute is the fourth track on Prince's thirtieth album
The Slaughterhouse released March 29, 2004. The lyrics refer to
Clive Davis' firing from Arista Records.

golden parachute
album: the slaughter house

1½ oz.	Whiskey
1 oz.	Dry Vermouth
1 oz.	Pineapple Juice

Serves 1

1. Shake with ice and strain into cocktail glass.

Graffiti Bridge is the sixteenth track on Prince's twelfth album Graffiti Bridge released August 20, 1990. The movie Graffiti Bridge was developed in September 1987, and ultimately released November 2, 1990.

graffiti bridge
album: graffiti bridge

| 1½ oz. | Gin |
| 1½ oz. | Sweet Vermouth |

Serves 1

1. Stir with ice and strain into cocktail glass.

Hot Thing is the eighth track on the first disc of Prince's ninth album Sign O' The Times released March 31, 1987, and was the b-side for the album's fourth single I Could Never Take the Place of Your Man released November 3, 1987 featuring two remixes by Shep Pettibone included on the 12" marking the first release of remixes by an outside producer on a Prince release.

hot thing
album: sign o' the times

1½ oz.	Gin
½	Lime Juiced
	Ginger Ale

Serves 1

1. Pour gin and lime juice over ice cubes in cocktail glass.

2. Fill with ginger ale.

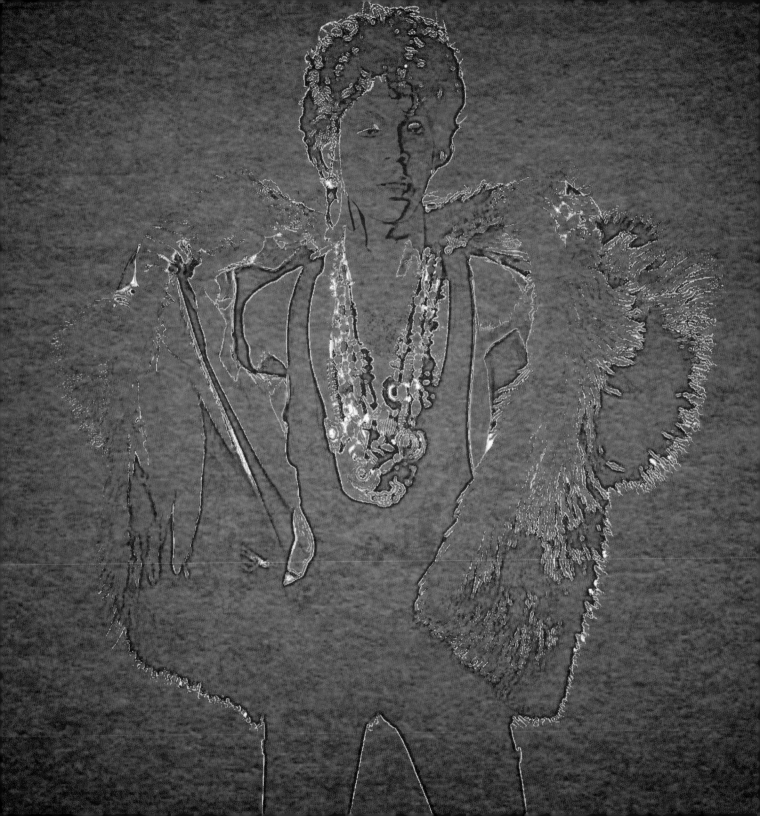

Housequake is the third track on the first disc of Prince's ninth album Sign O' The Times released March 31, 1987, and was the b-side for the album's third single U Got The Look released July 14, 1987. The track was initially placed as the second track on the album Camille and was planned as the b-side of the single Shockadelica (both credited to Camille). It was then included as the third track on the first disc on the triple-album Crystal Ball, which was pared down to become Sign O' The Times. Housequake (7 Minutes MoQuake) contains a sample from the song Crazay by Jesse Johnson featuring Sly Stone from the album Shockadelica (1986), after which Prince's song Shockadelica was named.

housequake
album: sign o' the times

1½ oz.	Gin
¾ oz.	Dry Vermouth
2 dashes	Orange Bitters
	Olive

Serves 1

1. Stir with ice and strain into cocktail glass.

2. Garnish with olive.

Hypnoparadise is the fifth track on Prince's thirtieth album
The Slaughterhouse released March 29, 2004, but initially released
July 7, 2001 part of NPG Music Club Edition #6 as a download.

hypnoparadise
album: the slaughterhouse

1½ oz.	Gin
1 dash	Angostura Bitters
¼ tsp.	Orange Juice
¼ tsp.	Pineapple Juice
¼ tsp.	Lemon Juice
½ tsp.	Powdered Sugar

Serves 1

1. Shake with ice and strain into cocktail glass.

i...incense and candles

Insatiable is the twelfth track on Prince's thirteenth album Diamonds and Pearls (Prince and the New Power Generation) released October 1, 1991, and was the album's third single released November 4, 1991.

insatiable
album: diamonds and pearls

1½ oz.	Gin
½ oz.	Dry Vermouth
½ oz.	Sweet Vermouth
1 dash	Angostura Bitters

Serves 1

1. Stir with ice and strain into cocktail glass.

International Lover is the eleventh track on Prince's fifth album 1999
released October 27, 1982. The track was intended for The Time's
second album What Time Is It?. A version with Morris Day on vocals
was recorded but Prince didn't like the result and reclaimed the song
to use on 1999. A solo piano rehearsal of the track was released in
September 2018 on Piano & A Microphone 1983, a posthumous album.
Prince recorded an initial version, with Morris Day on drums, as Take 1
(Live In Studio) released November 29, 2019 as the eighth track on
Disc 3: Vault Tracks 1 of the re-issue album 1999 (Super) Deluxe Edition.

international lover
album: 1999

1½ oz.	Gin
½ oz.	Dry Vermouth
½ oz.	Sweet Vermouth
	Lemon Peel Twist
	Olive

Serves 1

1. Stir over ice cubes vermouth and gin in a mixing glass.

2. Strain into cocktail glass.

3. Garnish with lemon peel twist and olive.

Irresistible Bitch is the eleventh track on disc three: The B-Sides of Prince's compilation album The Hits / The B-Sides released September 14, 1993, and was the b-side of Let's Pretend We're Married released November 16, 1983 the fourth single from the album 1999.

irresistible bitch
album: the hits/b-sides

1 oz.	Gin
1½ tsp.	Dry Vermouth
1½ tsp.	Sweet Vermouth
1 dash	Angostura Bitters
¼	Orange Juiced

Serves 1

1. Shake with ice and strain into cocktail glass.

Joy In Repetition is the eighth track on Prince's twelfth album
Graffiti Bridge released August 20, 1990.

joy in repetition
album: graffiti bridge

¾ oz.	Brandy
¾ oz.	Triple Sec
¾ oz.	Orange Juice

Serves 1

1. Shake with ice and strain into cocktail glass.

Judas Smile is the second track on Prince's twenty-ninth album
The Chocolate Invasion released March 29, 2004, and was part of the
NPG Music Club Edition #7 as a download released August 28, 2001.
The song was sampled in the extended version of Sexmesexmenot
also included on The Chocolate Invasion.

judas smile
album: the chocolate invasion

1 oz.	Gin
½ oz.	Dry Vermouth
½ oz.	Sweet Vermouth
1 dash	Angostura Bitters
¼ tsp.	Orange Juice

Serves 1

1. Shake with ice and strain into cocktail glass.

Jughead is the ninth track on Prince's thirteenth album Diamonds and Pearls (Prince and the New Power Generation) released October 1, 1991. Steve Fargnoli (Prince's former manager) sued Prince in December 1991 stating that the spoken word message about managers included at the end of the song was about him, and broke their non-disclosure agreement. The defamation and breach-of-contract suit demanded $5 million in damages.

jughead
album: diamonds and pearls

1½ oz.	Gin
1½ tsp.	Dry Vermouth
1½ tsp.	Sweet Vermouth
½ tsp.	Triple Sec
1 dash	Angostura Bitters
½ tsp.	Lemon Juice

Serves 1

1. Shake with ice and strain into cocktail glass.

Kiss is the tenth track on Prince's eighth album Parade (Prince and the Revolution) released March 31, 1986, and was the first single released February 5, 1986. The song was recorded initially by Prince as an acoustic blues-style demo for the band Mazarati. Prince heard Mazarati's recorded version and reclaimed the song, worked on it further omitting a bass guitar part and guitar solo, and added the signature guitar lick. Mazarati's Sir Casey Terry's vocals were also replaced with Prince's own in a higher octave, but Prince kept the original recording.

kiss
album: parade

¾ oz.	Brandy
¾ oz.	Gin
½	Egg White
1	Lemon Juiced

Serves 1

1. Shake with ice and strain into cocktail glass.

l...life 'o' the party

165

La, La, La, He, He, Hee is the thirteenth track on disc three:
The B-Sides of Prince's compilation album The Hits / The B-Sides
released September 14, 1993, and was the b-side of Sign O' The Times
released February 18, 1987 the first single from the album Sign O' The
Times. According to the liner notes, the song was created as a response
to a dare by Sheena Easton who claimed that Prince couldn't write a
song from such a basic phrase. The song was originally titled My Tree
but has nothing to do with his unreleased 1990 song My Tree.

la, la, la, he, he, hee
album: the hits / b-sides

¾ oz.	Gin
¾ oz.	Light Rum
1½ tsp.	Triple Sec
¼	Lemon Juiced

Serves 1

1. Shake with ice and strain into cocktail glass.

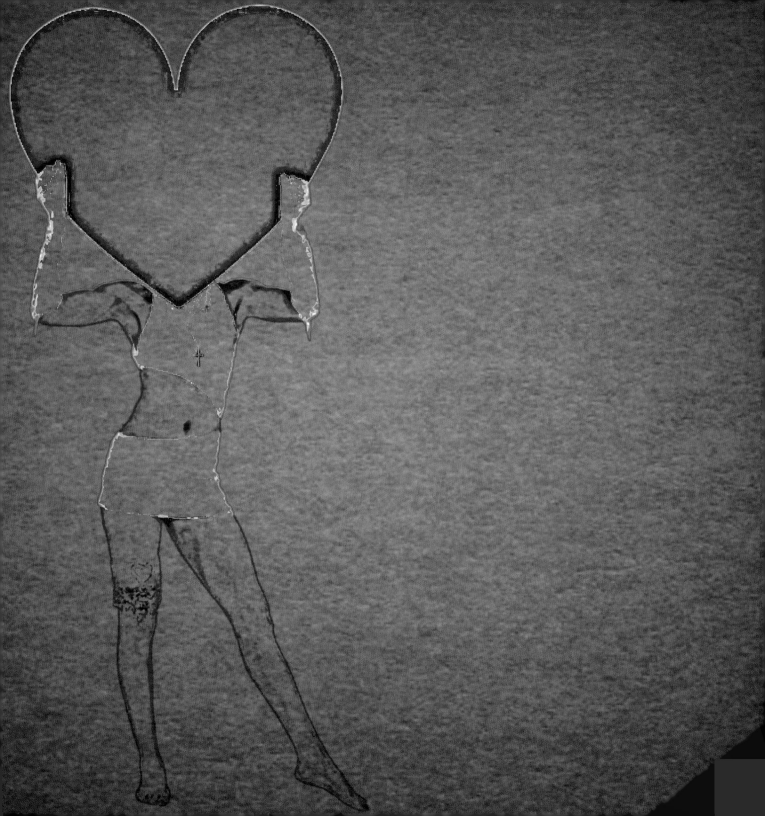

Lady Cab Driver is the ninth track on Prince's fifth album 1999 released
October 27, 1982.

lady cab driver
album: 1999

1½ oz.	Gin
1	Egg White
1 tsp.	Cream
1 tsp.	Powdered Sugar

Serves 1

1. Shake with ice and strain into cocktail glass.

Lavaux is the sixth track on Prince's thirty-fifth album 20Ten released July 10, 2010. The song is named after The Lavaux, a region in the canton of Vaud in Switzerland, in the district of Lavaux-Oron. This region is close to the site of the Montreux Jazz Festival, where Prince played shows in 2007 and 2009.

lavaux
album: 20ten

2 oz.	Gin
2 dashes	Orange Bitters
½ tsp.	Sugar Syrup
½ tsp.	Maraschino Juice
	Lemon Peel Twist

Serves 1

1. In saucepan, stir 1¼ cups sugar into ¾ cups hot water to make 1 cup of simple syrup.

2. Stir all ingredients with ice and strain into cocktail glass.

3. Garnish with lemon peel twist.

Le Grind is the first track on Prince's sixteenth album The Black Album released November 22, 1994. But, the album was widely bootlegged after its initial cancellation in 1987.

le grind
album: the black album

1 oz.	Gin
½ oz.	Triple Sec
1 tbsp.	Orange Juice
¼ oz.	Powdered Sugar

Serves 1

1. Shake with ice and strain into cocktail glass.

Lemon Crush is the seventh track on Prince's eleventh album Batman released June 20, 1989. The vocals on the album are attributed to Bruce Wayne, a character from the movie, as if Prince is singing on his behalf.

lemon crush
album: batman

1½ oz.	Tequila
½ oz.	Triple Sec
1 oz.	Lemon Juice
1 cup	Crushed Ice
	Lemon Slice

Serves 1

1. Crush ice in an electric blender.

2. Combine ingredients with crushed ice in electric blender.

3. Blend at low speed for five seconds.

4. Then, blend at high speed until firm.

5. Pour into cocktail glass.

6. Garnish with lemon slice.

Let's Go Crazy is the first track on Prince's sixth album Purple Rain (Prince and the Revolution), and was the album's second single released July 18, 1984.

let's go crazy
album: purple rain

¾ oz.	Scotch
¾ oz.	Dry Vermouth
¾ oz.	Grapefruit Juice

Serves 1

1. Shake with ice and strain into cocktail glass.

Lion Of Judah is the ninth track from Prince's thirty-second album Planet Earth released July 15, 2007. In Christian tradition, the Lion of Judah represents Jesus. Prince's use of the phrase refers to its use in Revelation 5:5.

lion of judah
album: planet earth

1½ oz.	Vodka
¾ oz.	Dry Vermouth
	Lemon Peel Twist

Serves 1

1. Shake with ice and strain into cocktail glass.

2. Garnish with lemon peel twist.

Little Red Corvette is the second track on Prince's fifth album 1999 released October 27, 1982, and was the album's second single released February 9, 1983.

little red corvette
album: 1999

| 1½ oz. | Light Rum |
| 1½ oz. | Sweet Vermouth |

Serves 1

1. Stir with ice and strain into cocktail glass.

Lotusflow3r is the thirty-third full-length album by Prince released March 24, 2009, and was initially released as a download on the launch date of Prince's website lotusflow3r.com. A CD was released March 29, 2009 exclusively at Target retail stores.

lotusflow3r
album: lotusflow3r

1 oz.	Gin
½ oz.	Dry Vermouth
½ oz.	Sweet Vermouth
¼	Orange Juiced
	Orange Slice

Serves 1

1. Shake with ice and strain into cocktail glass.

2. Garnish with orange slice.

Love 2 The 9's is the third track on Prince's fourteenth album ☩ (Prince and the New Power Generation) released October 13, 1992. The track features a spoken dialogue by Mayte, marking her first appearance on a Prince-related track. The lyrics mention listening to a band playing "new power soul," a phrase first used in 1988; and refer to "joy fantastic," a phrase first used by Prince in the song Rave Un2 The Joy Fantastic recorded in 1988 but not released until 1999.

love 2 the 9's
album: love symbol

2 oz.	Gin
¼ oz.	Dry Vermouth
	Lemon Peel Twist
	Olive

Serves 1

1. Stir over ice cubes vermouth and gin.

2. Strain into cocktail glass.

3. Garnish with lemon peel twist and olive.

Lovesexy is the sixth track on Prince's tenth album Lovesexy released May 10, 1988. A live performance was included on the Lovesexy Live 1 VHS released April 19, 1989 from the September 9, 1988 live TV broadcast. Prince described the term "lovesexy" on tour as "the feeling u get when u fall in love - not with a girl or boy, but with the heavens above," a lyric not present in the song itself but taken from the song Luv Sexy from which Lovesexy materialized.

lovesexy
album: lovesexy

2 oz.	Gin
1	Egg White
2 tsp.	Cream
½	Lemon Juiced
1 tsp.	Powdered Sugar
2	Ice Cubes
	Carbonated Water

Serves 1

1. Shake with ice and strain over two ice cubes into cocktail glass.

2. Fill with carbonated water and stir.

Magnificent is a "virtual b-side" to Musicology released April 5, 2004, the first single from Prince's twenty-eighth album Musicology.

magnificent
virtual: "virtual b-side" to musicology

1½ oz.	Gin
¾ oz.	Sweet Vermouth
1 dash	Angostura Bitters

Serves 1

1. Stir with ice and strain into cocktail glass.

Man'O'War (a.k.a. Man 'O' War) is the eleventh track on Prince's twenty-third album Rave Un2 The Joy Fantastic released November 9, 1999, and was available in early 2000 as a promotional release. A remixed version was included as the eighth track on the companion album Rave In2 The Joy Fantastic released April 30, 2001.

man 'o' war
album: rave un2 the joy fantastic / rave in2 the joy fantastic

1½ oz.	Whiskey
1½ tsp.	Dry Vermouth
1½ tsp.	Sweet Vermouth
1 tbsp.	Lemon Juice

Serves 1

1. Shake with ice and strain into cocktail glass.

Mellow is the seventh track on Prince's twenty-fourth album The Rainbow Children released November 20, 2001, his first album after reverting back to the name Prince. Initially, the album was released October 16, 2001 as an NPG Music Club download. The track was offered as a free download from AOL.com to AOL members on January 14, 2002. The song's lyrics refer to "The Egg," a building on the grounds of Paisley Park Studios.

mellow
album: the rainbow children

1¼ oz.	Brandy
1¼ oz.	Sweet Vermouth
1 dash	Angostura Bitters
½ tsp.	Sugar Syrup

Serves 1

1. In saucepan, stir 1¼ cups sugar into ¾ cups hot water to make 1 cup of simple syrup.

2. Stir all ingredients with ice and strain into cocktail glass.

Melody Cool is the fourteenth track on Prince's twelfth album
Graffiti Bridge released August 20, 1990, and was the album's third
single released December 4, 1990. The track is featured with a different
mix and included on Mavis Staples' album The Voice released in 1993,
and on the 1995 re-release.

melody cool
album: graffiti bridge

1 oz.	Gin
½ oz.	Dry Vermouth
½ oz.	Sweet Vermouth
1 dash	Angostura Bitters
¼	Orange Juiced

Serves 1

1. Shake with ice and strain into cocktail glass.

Movie Star is the ninth track on the first disc of Prince's twentieth album Crystal Ball released January 29, 1998. The Crystal Ball liner notes state that the song was chosen for inclusion because it was "D'Angelo's favorite bootleg," and also state that the song was written for The Time. The version released on Crystal Ball contains an opening which samples Jam of the Year in the background of a party scene.

movie star
album: crystal ball

1½ oz.	Gin
¾ oz.	Dry Vermouth
	Lemon Peel Twist
	Olive

Serves 1

1. Stir over ice cubes vermouth and gin.

2. Strain into cocktail glass.

3. Garnish with lemon peel twist and olive.

Mr. Goodnight is the sixth track from Prince's thirty-second album Planet Earth released July 15, 2007, and was the b-side of the promotional single Chelsea Rodgers released August 6, 2007.

mr. goodnight
album: planet earth

1½ oz.	Gin
1 tsp.	Orange Juice
¼ tsp.	Lemon Juice
1 lump	Sugar
4	Mint Sprigs

Serves 1

1. Muddle sugar lump with mint sprigs, lemon juice, orange juice, and gin.

2. Shake with ice and strain into cocktail glass.

Mr. Happy is the eleventh track on the first disc of Prince's nineteenth album Emancipation released November 19, 1996. It contains a repeated sample of "bought a house next to Prince," taken from What Can I Do? by Ice Cube.

mr. happy
album: emancipation

1½ oz.	Gin
¾ oz.	Triple Sec
1 dash	Orange Bitters

Serves 1

1. Shake with ice and strain into cocktail glass.

Muse 2 The Pharaoh is the second track on Prince's twenty-fourth album The Rainbow Children released November 20, 2001, his first album after reverting back to the name Prince. Initially, the album was released October 16, 2001 as an NPG Music Club download.

muse 2 the pharaoh
album: the rainbow children

1½ oz.	Gin
½ oz.	Triple Sec
1 oz.	Lemon Juice

Serves 1

1. Shake with ice and strain into cocktail glass.

My Medallion is the fifth track on Prince's twenty-ninth album
The Chocolate Invasion initially released March 29, 2004. The album
version with the track My Medallion was released December 3, 2015,
using the original unissued 2003 configuration. The track was initially
released in 2001 as a download part of NPG Music Club Edition #8.
The music is based on Eric Burdon and War's 1970 song Spill The Wine.

my medallion
album: the chocolate invasion

1 oz.	Gin
1 oz.	Sweet Vermouth
	Lemon Peel Twist
	Olive

Serves 1

1. Stir over ice cubes vermouth and gin.

2. Strain into cocktail glass.

3. Garnish with lemon peel twist and olive.

New Power Generation (Pt. 1) is the second track on Prince's twelfth album Graffiti Bridge released August 20, 1990, and was the album's third single released October 23, 1990. New Power Generation (Pt. II) is the seventeenth track on the album, and was the b-side of the New Power Generation single. The initial song was titled Bold Generation recorded January 12, 1982, and features only Prince and Morris Day. Bold Generation is the sixth track on Disc 3: Vault Tracks 1 of the re-issue album 1999 (Super) Deluxe Edition released November 29, 2019.

new power generation
album: graffiti bridge

1½ oz.	Light Rum
1 dash	Angostura Bitters
1 oz.	Grapefruit Juice
1	Lime Juiced
3 tsp.	Powdered Sugar

Serves 1

1. Shake with ice and strain into cocktail glass.

o...one nite alone...

213

Orgasm (a.k.a. Poem) is the tenth track on Prince's fifteenth
album Come released August 16, 1994. The track reuses a guitar solo
from Private Joy and vocals from Vanity 6's unreleased track Vibrator.
The "poem" was based on lines adapted from the Old Testament book
Song of Songs (a.k.a the Song of Solomon). For the final configuration
of the album, the track was renamed Orgasm and portions of the
"poem" were distributed as opening segments of other tracks.

orgasm
album: come

1 oz.	Gin
1 oz.	Orange Juice
¼ tsp.	Powdered Sugar

Serves 1

1. Shake with ice and strain into cocktail glass.

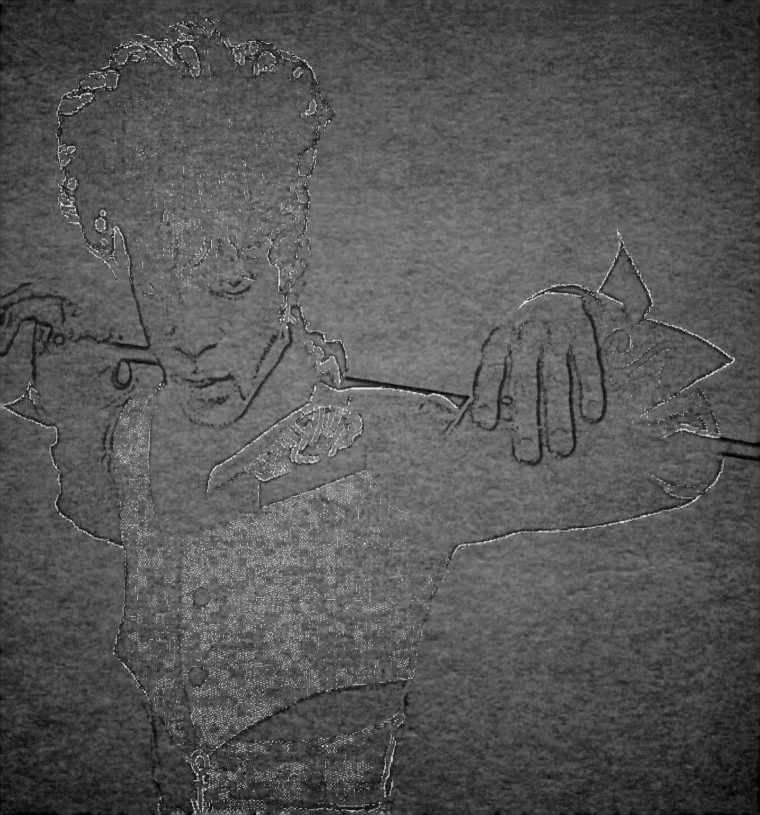

Paisley Park is the second track on Prince's seventh album Around The World In A Day (Prince and the Revolution) released April 22, 1985. Paisley Park became the name of Prince's recording studio complex, Paisley Park Studios, when it opened in 1987. Prince had previously used the term "Paisley Park" to refer to the recording facility at Flying Cloud Drive Warehouse in Eden Prairie, MN. The name was also used as his record label, Paisley Park Records from 1985 to 1993. Despite the many uses of the term, the song's lyrics state that "Paisley Park is in your heart."

paisley park
album: around the world in a day

1½ oz.	Gin
¾ oz.	Sweet Vermouth
1 tbsp.	Pineapple Juice

Serves 1

1. Stir with ice and strain into cocktail glass.

Partyman is the fourth track on Prince's eleventh album Batman released June 20, 1989, and was the album's third single released August 25, 1989. The vocals are attributed to The Joker, a character from the movie, as if Prince is singing on his behalf. The track replaced Rave Un2 The Joy Fantastic as the background music of the museum scene in the movie Batman, in which The Joker traps and then 'serenades' Vicki Vale.

partyman
album: batman

¾ oz.	Gin
¾ oz.	Dry Vermouth
2 dashes	Angostura Bitters
¾ oz.	Orange Juice

Serves 1

1. Shake with ice and strain into cocktail glass.

Pheromone is the third track on Prince's fifteenth album Come released August 16, 1994. An instrumental version of the track was used as the theme music for BET's Video LP show in April 1993. During a Love4oneanother.com "? of the week" in 1999, a fan using the name CTM asked where the story/lyrics for the song came from, to which Prince replied, "Carmen Electra and The Crazy Horse." Presumably, Le Crazy Horse Saloon (Le Crazy Horse de Paris), a Parisian cabaret known for its stage shows performed by nude female dancers and the diverse range of magic and variety 'turns' between each nude show.

pheromone
album: come

1½ oz.	Gin
1½ tsp.	Dry Vermouth
1½ tsp.	Sweet Vermouth
1 dash	Angostura Bitters

Serves 1

1. Stir with ice and strain into cocktail glass.

Play In The Sunshine is the second track on the first disc of Prince's ninth album Sign O' The Times released March 31, 1987.

play in the sunshine
album: sign o' the times

1½ oz.	Gin
¾ oz.	Sweet Vermouth
1 dash	Angostura Bitters
	Orange Peel Twist

Serves 1

1. Stir with ice and strain into cocktail glass.

2. Garnish with orange peel twist.

Plectrumelectrum is the fourth track on Prince's thirty-sixth album Plectrumelectrum (Prince and 3rdEyeGirl) released September 30, 2014. The track is an instrumental composed by Donna Grantis, originally released by her Donna Grantis Electric Band's 2012 album Suites, under the name Elektra (Elektra Suite).

plectrumelectrum
album: plectrumelectrum

1½ oz.	Light Rum
1½ oz.	Dry Vermouth
2 dashes	Angostura Bitters

Serves 1

1. Stir with ice and strain into cocktail glass.

Poom Poom is the third track on disc three of Prince's twentieth album Crystal Ball released January 29, 1998. The track premiered in The New Power Generation Stores in London and Minneapolis on June 7, 1995 to celebrate Prince's 37th birthday, stated as ♀'s 2nd birthday.

poompoom
album: crystal ball

1 oz.	Gin
½ oz.	Dry Vermouth
1 oz.	Grapefruit Juice

Serves 1

1. Shake with ice and strain into cocktail glass.

Positivity is the ninth track on Prince's tenth album Lovesexy released May 10, 1988. In 1993, a newly-recorded version by Mavis Staples was included on her album The Voice and re-released in 1995. An unreleased version contains a rap by Cat, sampled from Cindy C. when "The Black Album" was aborted. Prince was unaware at the time the rap was taken from J.M. Silk's 1985 track Music Is The Key and ultimately removed the rap.

positivity
album: lovesexy

1 oz.	Dry Vermouth
1 oz.	Sweet Vermouth
1 dash	Orange Bitters

Serves 1

1. Stir with ice and strain into cocktail glass.

Power Fantastic is the twentieth track on disc three: The B-Sides of Prince's compilation album The Hits / The B-Sides released September 14, 1993. The song was based on a track called Carousel written by Wendy Melvoin and Lisa Coleman in 1985. Prince developed a melody and wrote lyrics for the song. The song was mentioned in an early draft of Graffiti Bridge where Power Fantastic was supposed to be sung by the character "Ruthie Washington," who Prince hoped would be played by Madonna.

power fantastic
album: the hits/b-sides

2 oz.	Gin
1	Egg White
¼	Lemon Juiced

Serves 1

1. Shake with ice and strain into cocktail glass.

Prettyman is the eighteenth track on Prince's twenty-third album Rave Un2 The Joy Fantastic released November 9, 1999, as a hidden track. An extended version was included as the fourteenth track on the remix companion album Rave In2 The Joy Fantastic released April 30, 2001, also as a hidden track.

prettyman
album: rave un2 the joy fantastic / rave in2 the joy fantastic

¾ oz.	Gin
¾ oz.	Sweet Vermouth
¾ oz.	Dry Vermouth
	Pineapple Strip or Ring

Serves 1

1. Shake with ice and strain into cocktail glass.

2. Garnish with pineapple strip or ring.

Private Joy is the fourth track on Prince's fourth album Controversy released October 14, 1981, and was the b-side of Do Me, Baby the album's third single released July 16, 1982.

private joy
album: controversy

1½ oz.	Light Rum
¾ oz.	Pineapple Juice
½ tsp.	Lemon Juice

Serves 1

1. Shake with ice and strain into cocktail glass.

Purple Rain is the ninth track on Prince's sixth album Purple Rain (Prince and the Revolution) released June 25, 1984, and was the third single released September 26, 1984.

purple rain
album: purple rain

1½ oz.	Vodka
3 oz.	Grape Juice
3 oz.	Grapefruit Juice
	Sugar

Serves 1

1. Chill and stir.

2. Add sugar to taste.

3. Serve in a cocktail glass.

q...the question of u

The Question of U is the fourth track on Prince's twelfth album
Graffiti Bridge released August 20, 1990.

the question of u
album: graffiti bridge

¾ oz.	Gin
¾ oz.	Dry Vermouth
¾ oz.	Sweet Vermouth

Serves 1

1. Shake with ice and strain into cocktail glass.

r...ripopgodazippa

245

Raspberry Beret is the fourth track on Prince's seventh album
Around The World In A Day (Prince and the Revolution) released
April 22, 1985.

raspberry beret
album: around the world in a day

2 oz.	Gin
1 tsp.	Raspberry Syrup
¾ oz.	Cream

Serves 1

1. In saucepan, stir 1¼ cups sugar and 1 cup fresh/frozen raspberries into ¾ cups hot water to make 1 cup of raspberry syrup.

2. Shake all ingredients with ice and strain into cocktail glass.

Rave Un2 The Joy Fantastic (a.k.a. Rave Unto The Joy Fantastic) is the first track on Prince's twenty-third album Rave Un2 The Joy Fantastic released November 9, 1999. A remixed version with additional lyrics titled Rave In2 The Joy Fantastic was included as the first track on the remix companion album Rave In2 The Joy Fantastic released April 30, 2001. The song was replaced with Partyman in a scene in the Batman movie. Samples from the chorus appear both in the songs Batdance and 200 Balloons.

rave un2 the joy fantastic
album: rave un2 the joy fantastic / rave in2 the joy fantastic

5 parts	Light Rum
1 dash	Dry Vermouth
	Lemon Twist

Serves 1

1. Serve on the rocks in a cocktail glass.

2. Garnish with lemon twist.

Reflection is the twelfth track on Prince's twenty-eighth album Musicology released April 20, 2004. But, the album was initially released March 27, 2004 as a concert giveaway. The track was offered as a download to NPG Music Club members May 29, 2003. Prince and Wendy Melvoin performed the song on The Tavis Smiley Show on February 12, 2004.

reflection
album: musicology

1½ oz.	Gin
¾ oz.	Dry Vermouth
1 dash	Orange Bitters

Serves 1

1. Stir with ice and strain into cocktail glass.

Ripopgodazippa is the fourth track on disc one of Prince's twentieth album Crystal Ball released January 29, 1998. The song was featured in the Paul Verhoeven-directed movie Showgirls three years before its release, but not included on the movie's soundtrack.

ripopgodazippa
album: crystal ball

2 oz.	Gin
½ tsp.	Triple Sec
1	Egg White
1 tbsp.	Cream
½	Lemon Juiced
1 tsp.	Powdered Sugar
2	Ice Cubes
	Carbonated Water

Serves 1

1. Shake with ice and strain over two ice cubes into cocktail glass.

2. Fill with carbonated water and stir.

Ronnie, Talk to Russia is the fifth track on Prince's fourth album
Controversy released October 14, 1981, and was the b-side
of Let's Work the album's second single released January 6, 1982.
The title and lyrics of the song refer to Ronald Reagan, the 40th
President of the United States of America.

ronnie, talk to russia
album: controversy

1½ oz.	Scotch
¾ oz.	Sweet Vermouth
	Pineapple Strip or Ring

Serves 1

1. Stir with ice and strain into cocktail glass.

2. Garnish with pineapple strip or ring.

Sarah is the ninth track on Prince's twenty-second album
The Vault: Old Friends 4 Sale released August 24, 1999.

sarah
album: the vault: old friends 4 sale

1 oz.	Gin
1½ tsp.	Light Rum
1½ tsp.	Triple Sec
1 tbsp.	Grapefruit Juice
1 tbsp.	Lemon Juice

Serves 1

1. Shake with ice and strain into cocktail glass.

Scandalous is the eighth track on Prince's eleventh album Batman released June 20, 1989. Scandalous! (the title with an exclamation mark) was released as the album's fourth single November 28, 1989. Prince's father, John L. Nelson, is credited as a co-writer. Scandalous is attributed to Batman. The song was re-worked to a three-part version called The Scandalous Sex Suite—including the three parts titled The Crime, The Passion and The Rapture. Actress Kim Basinger, who played the character Vicki Vale in the Batman movie, took part in the sessions, which were released on the Scandalous! maxi-single December 1, 1989, also known as the The Scandalous Sex Suite EP.

scandalous
album: batman

1 oz.	Scotch
½ oz.	Dry Vermouth
½ tsp.	Triple Sec
1 tbsp.	Orange Juice
¼ tsp.	Powdered Sugar
	Lemon Peel Twist

Serves 1

1. Shake with ice and strain into cocktail glass.

2. Garnish with lemon peel twist.

Scarlet Pussy is the twelfth track on disc three: The B-Sides of Prince's compilation album The Hits / The B-Sides released September 14, 1993, and was the b-side of I Wish U Heaven released September 20, 1988 the third single from Prince's tenth album Lovesexy. The song was credited to Camille, but was initially planned for Sheila E. as the song also features her vocals. The style and lyrics are reminiscent of George Clinton's Parliament and Funkadelic. The line "Pussycat, pussycat, wherefore art thou, puppy?" is a reference to the line "Romeo, Romeo, wherefore art thou, Romeo?" from William Shakespeare's 16th century play Romeo and Juliet.

scarlet pussy
album: the hits / the b-sides

1½ oz.	Gin
1½ tsp.	Dry Vermouth
1½ tsp.	Sweet Vermouth
	Lemon Slice

Serves 1

1. Stir with ice and strain into cocktail glass.

2. Garnish with lemon slice.

Sex in the Summer is the first track on disc two of Prince's nineteenth album Emancipation released November 19, 1996. The track features a loop of the ultrasound heartbeat of Prince and Mayte's unborn child "Amiir." The album's liner notes state that the original title of the track was Conception.

sex in the summer
album: emancipation

1½ oz.	Gin
1½ tsp.	Sweet Vermouth
1½ tsp.	Grapefruit Juice

Serves 1

1. Shake with ice and strain into cocktail glass.

Sexmesexmenot (a.k.a. Sex Me Sex Me Not) is the fifth track on Prince's twenty-ninth album The Chocolate Invasion released March 29, 2004, and the eighth track on the 2015 release. The track was part of the NPG Music Club Edition #5 as a download June 11, 2001. The Chocolate Invasion's version includes samples and spoken quotations from Judas Smile.

sexmesexmenot
album: the chocolate invasion

1½ oz.	Gin
1½ oz.	Dry Vermouth

Serves 1

1. Stir with ice and strain into cocktail glass.

Sexual Suicide is the seventh track on disc two of Prince's twentieth album Crystal Ball released January 29, 1998. The liner notes state that Sheila E. showed Prince how to play the drumbeat, but she is not given any writing credit.

sexual suicide
album: crystal ball

1½ oz.	Gin
1 dash	Orange Bitters
1 oz.	Lemon Juice
1½ tsp.	Maple Syrup

Serves 1

1. Shake with ice and strain into cocktail glass.

Sexy Dancer is the third track on Prince's second album, self-titled, Prince released October 19, 1979, and was a UK single released April 11, 1980. The song was the first Prince single released outside the United States that was not released as a single stateside.

sexy dancer
album: prince

2 oz.	Light Rum
1 tsp.	Triple Sec

Serves 1

1. Stir with ice and strain into cocktail glass.

Sexy MF is the second track on Prince's fourteenth album ♀
(Prince and the New Power Generation) released October 13, 1992,
and was the album's first single released June 30, 1992.

sexy mf
album: love symbol

1 oz.	Brandy
½ oz.	Triple Sec
¼	Lemon Juiced

Serves 1

1. Shake with ice and strain into cocktail glass.

Shockadelica is the tenth track on disc three: The B-Sides of Prince's compilation album The Hits / The B-Sides released September 14, 1993, and was initially the b-side of If I Was Your Girlfriend released May 6, 1987 the second single from Prince's ninth album Sign O' The Times. Prince wrote the track after hearing that Jesse Johnson's forthcoming album was titled Shockadelica but had no title track. Prince felt that every album with a great title should contain a title track. Prince sent the finished song to Jesse Johnson, and Minneapolis' radio station KMOJ where the song premiered a few weeks before Jesse Johnson's album was released.

shockadelica
album: the hits / the b-sides

1½ oz.	Gin
¾ oz.	Orange Juice
¼ tsp.	Powdered Sugar

Serves 1

1. Shake with ice and strain into cocktail glass.

Soft and Wet is the third track on Prince's debut album For You released April 7, 1978, and was the album's first single released June 7, 1978. This was Prince's first single.

soft and wet
album: for you

2 oz.	Gin
½ tsp.	Triple Sec
2 dashes	Orange Bitters
	Lemon peel Twist

Serves 1

1. Stir with ice and strain into cocktail glass.

2. Garnish with lemon peel twist.

Solo is the eighth track on Prince's fifteenth album Come released August 16, 1994. The lyrics are written by David Henry Hwang, writer of the play M. Butterfly. Prince asked Hwang to write a poem "about loss" to use as a spoken word interlude in a song. Hwang wrote Solo as a poem and faxed it to Paisley Park Studios. A few days later, Hwang received a cassette containing the full song, with the lyrics sung rather than as a spoken interlude.

solo
album: come

1 oz.	Gin
1 tbsp.	Lemon Juice
1 tbsp.	Orange Juice
	Pineapple Strip or Ring

Serves 1

1. Shake with ice and strain into cocktail glass.

2. Garnish with pineapple strip or ring.

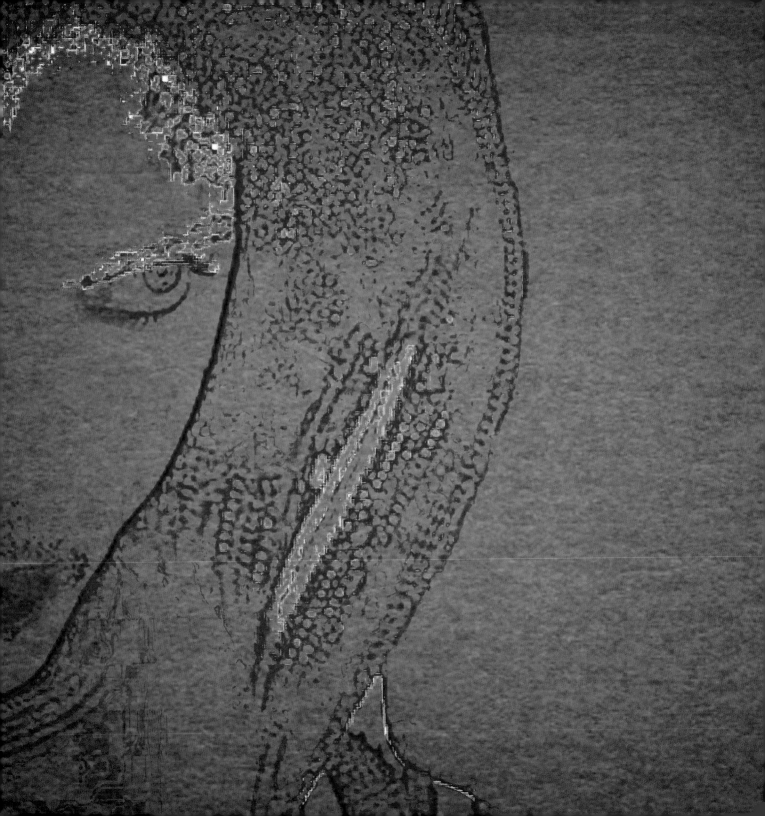

Soul Sanctuary is the third track on disc two of Prince's nineteenth album Emancipation released November 19, 1996. The song was originally written by Sandra St. Victor, Johnny Kemp and Tom Hammer as Sanctuary, and sent to Prince in Spring 1995 following a loose agreement for Prince and Sandra St. Victor to work together.

soul sanctuary
album: emancipation

1½ oz.	Brandy
1½ oz.	Gin
2 dashes	Angostura Bitters
½ tsp.	Sugar Syrup
	Lemon Peel Twist

Serves 1

1. In saucepan, stir 1¼ cups sugar into ¾ cups hot water to make 1 cup of simple syrup.

2. Stir with ice and strain into cocktail glass.

3. Garnish with lemon peel twist.

Supercute is the third track on Prince's twenty-ninth album The Chocolate Invasion initially released March 29, 2004. The track was a stand-alone single sold only at concerts on Prince's Hit N Run Tour beginning April 14, 2001. The song was included in the NPG Music Club Edition #5 as a download.

supercute
album: the chocolate invasion

1½ oz.	Gin
½ oz.	Dry Vermouth
½ oz.	Triple Sec
	Lemon Peel Twist

Serves 1

1. Shake with ice and strain into cocktail glass.

2. Garnish with lemon peel twist.

Superfunkycalifragisexy is the sixth track on Prince's sixteenth album The Black Album released November 22, 1994. The title is a spoof of the song Supercalifragilisticexpialidocious in the movie Mary Poppins (1964).

superfunkycalifragisexy
album: the black album

1½ oz.	Gin
½	Lemon Juiced
1 tsp.	Powdered Sugar
	Mint Sprigs

Serves 1

1. Shake with ice and strain into cocktail glass.

2. Garnish with mint sprigs.

Sweet Baby is the ninth track on Prince's fourteenth album ⚥
(Prince and the New Power Generation) released October 13, 1992.
The album is often referred to as Symbol or Love Symbol. It would later
become Prince's name in 1993, and under that name he released six
albums from 1995–1999.

sweet baby
album: love symbol

1 oz.	Gin
½ oz.	Triple Sec
1 tbsp.	Orange Juice

Serves 1

1. Shake with ice and strain into cocktail glass.

t...temptation

Tangerine is the sixth track on Prince's twenty-third album Rave Un2 The Joy Fantastic released November 9, 1999. An extended version was included as the fifth track on the remix companion album Rave In2 The Joy Fantastic released April 30, 2001.

tangerine
album: rave un2 the joy fantastic / rave in2 the joy fantastic

1 oz.	Gin
½ oz.	Dry Vermouth
½ oz.	Sweet Vermouth
½ tsp.	Triple Sec
1 tbsp.	Orange Juice

Serves 1

1. Shake with ice and strain into cocktail glass.

Te Amo Corazón is the third track on Prince's thirty-first album 3121 released March 21, 2006, and was the first single released December 13, 2005. The music video was shot in Marrakesh and stars Mia Maestro, and was directed by actress Salma Hayek.

te amo corazón
album: 3121

1½ oz.	Tequila
½ oz.	Dry Vermouth
1 dash	Angostura Bitters
	Lemon Peel Twist
	Olive

Serves 1

1. Stir with ice and strain into cocktail glass.

2. Garnish with lemon peel twist and olive.

Temptation is the ninth track on Prince's seventh album Around The World In A Day (Prince and the Revolution) released April 22, 1985.

temptation
album: around the world in a day

1½ oz.	Brandy
1	Egg Yolk
1 tsp.	Powdered Sugar

Serves 1

1. Shake with ice and strain into cocktail glass.

Thunder is the first track on Prince's thirteenth album Diamonds and
Pearls (Prince and the New Power Generation) released October 1, 1991.

thunder
album: diamonds and pearls

1½ oz.	Brandy
1	Egg Yolk
1 tsp.	Powdered Sugar
1 pinch	Cayenne Pepper

Serves 1

1. Shake with ice and strain into cocktail glass.

Tick, Tick, Bang is the tenth track on Prince's twelfth album
Graffiti Bridge released August 20, 1990. The song uses
a sample of Little Miss Lover by The Jimi Hendrix Experience
from the album Axis: Bold As Love (1969).

tick, tick, bang
album: graffiti bridge

¾ oz.	Brandy
¾ oz.	Gin
¾ oz.	Whiskey

Serves 1

1. Shake with ice and strain into cocktail glass.

Under The Cherry Moon is the fourth track on Prince's eighth album Parade (Prince and the Revolution) released March 31, 1986, and was the title of his second film. Although titled Parade "Music from the motion picture Under The Cherry Moon," the album is the film's official soundtrack. The song was performed live as an instrumental during the Purple Rain Tour.

under the cherry moon
album: parade

2 oz.	Gin
¼ tsp.	Lemon Juice
¼ tsp.	Maraschino Juice
	Maraschino Cherry

Serves 1

1. Shake with ice and strain into cocktail glass.

2. Garnish with cherry.

Underneath the Cream is the fourth track on Prince's twenty-ninth album The Chocolate Invasion released March 29, 2004. The song was included in the NPG Music Club Edition #10 as a download. "Underneath the cream" is a phrase mentioned on the original recording of Hot Wit U.

underneath the cream
album: the chocolate invasion

2 oz.	Light Rum
1 oz.	Cream
½ tsp.	Powdered Sugar
2	Ice Cubes
	Carbonated Water

Serves 1

1. Shake with ice and strain over two ice cubes into cocktail glass.

2. Fill with carbonated water and stir.

Uptown is the fifth track on Prince's third album Dirty Mind
released October 8, 1980. "Uptown" refers to a Minneapolis,
Minnesota, neighborhood around the Uptown Theater (Hennepin
and Lagoon Avenues). "Uptown" was Calhoun Square, for which
Prince wrote the song Calhoun Square, and the location of his
New Power Generation Store.

uptown
album: dirty mind

1½ oz.	Whiskey
¾ oz.	Dry Vermouth or Sweet Vermouth
	Olive

Serves 1

1. Stir with ice and strain into cocktail glass.

2. Garnish with olive.

v...vavoom

309

Valentina is the sixth track on Prince's thirty-fourth album MPLSoUND released March 24, 2009. The song is dedicated to actress Salma Hayek's young daughter, and also mentions actress Penelope Cruz in a play on words, "If Penelope wanna cruise...."

valentina
album: mplsound

1½ oz.	Tequila
½ oz.	Triple Sec
1 oz.	Lime Juice
	Lime Rind
	Salt

Serves 1

1. Rub rim of cocktail glass with rind of lime.

2. Dip rim in salt.

3. Shake ingredients with ice and strain into salt-rimmed glass.

Vavoom is the sixth track on Prince's twenty-ninth album The Chocolate Invasion released March 29, 2004, and was initially released from the NPG Music Club Edition #10 as a download.

vavoom

album: the chocolate invasion

2 oz.	Brandy
1 dash	Scotch
½ oz.	Sweet Vermouth
3 dashes	Angostura Bitters

Serves 1

1. Stir with ice and strain into cocktail glass.

Venus de Milo is the seventh track on Prince's eighth album Parade (Prince and the Revolution) released March 31, 1986.

venus de milo
album: parade

1 oz.	Dry Vermouth
1 oz.	Sweet Vermouth
1 dash	Orange Bitters

Serves 1

1. Stir with ice and strain into cocktail glass.

w...we can fuck

317

Wall of Berlin is the ninth track on Prince's thirty-third album Lotusflow3r released March 24, 2009.

wall of berlin
album: lotusflow3r

1½ oz.	Scotch
1 tbsp.	Orange Juice
1 tbsp.	Lemon Juice

Serves 1

1. Shake with ice and strain into cocktail glass.

White Mansion is the eighth track on disc one of Prince's nineteenth album Emancipation released November 19, 1996.

white mansion
album: emancipation

1½ oz.	Vodka
1 oz.	Lime Juice
1 tsp.	Powdered Sugar

Serves 1

1. Shake with ice and strain into cocktail glass.

Whitecaps is the fifth track on Prince's thirty-sixth album Plectrumelectrum (Prince and 3rdEyeGirl) released September 30, 2014. The track features lead vocals by 3rdEyeGirl drummer Hannah Ford.

whitecaps
album: plectrumelectrum

1½ oz.	Gin
1 oz.	Sweet Vermouth
1	Egg White

Serves 1

1. Shake with ice and strain into cocktail glass.

x...xtraloveable

325

X's Face is the seventh track on Prince's thirty-eighth album HitnRun Phase One released September 7, 2015. The track as The X's Face was available as a free download, emailed by Live Nation to ticket holders for four Prince and 3rdEyeGirl concerts scheduled in Louisville, KY, USA on March 14–15, 2015.

x's face
album: hitnrun phase one

1½ oz.	Gin
1 oz.	Sweet Vermouth
	Lemon Peel Twist

Serves 1

1. Stir with ice and strain into cocktail glass.

2. Garnish with lemon peel twist.

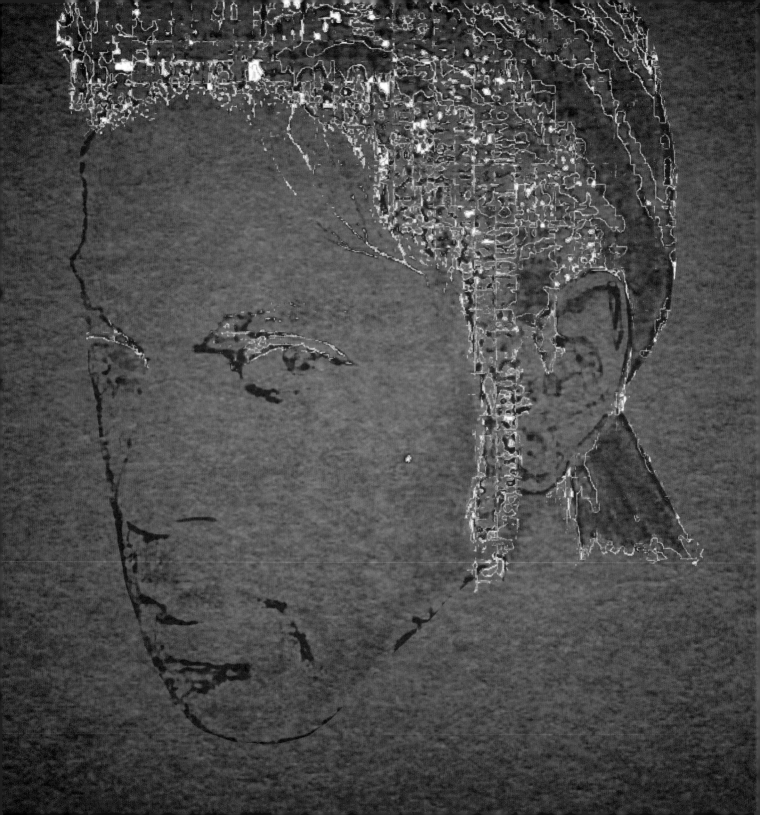

Xotica is the fifth track on Prince's twenty-sixth album Xpectation released January 1, 2003. The song was included as the sixth track on the album Xenophobia before the title track was removed and the album renamed Xpectation.

xotica
album: xpectation

¾ oz.	Gin
¾ oz.	Triple Sec
1 tbsp.	Pineapple Juice

Serves 1

1. Shake with ice and strain into cocktail glass.

Xtraloveable is the sixth track on Prince's thirty-ninth and final album HitnRun Phase Two released December 12, 2015. The track as Extraloveable was released as a single November 23, 2011. While the recording was new, the original track was recorded on April 3, 1982.

xtraloveable
album: hitnrun phase two

1 oz.	Light Rum
½ oz.	Triple Sec
1 tbsp.	Lemon Juice

Serves 1

1. Shake with ice and strain into cocktail glass.

y...yes

333

Young and Beautiful is the ninth track on Prince's twenty-fifth album
One Nite Alone.... released May 14, 2002.

young and beautiful
album: one nite alone... (solo piano & voice)

1 oz.	Gin
½ oz.	Dry Vermouth
½ oz.	Sweet Vermouth
1 tbsp.	Orange Juice
1	Onion Ring Slice

Serves 1

1. Shake with ice and strain into cocktail glass.

2. Garnish with onion ring slice.

z...zannalee

337

Zannalee is the sixth track on Prince's eighteenth album
Chaos and Disorder released July 9, 1996.

zannalee
album: chaos and disorder

1½ oz.	Scotch
½ oz.	Dry Vermouth
½ oz.	Sweet Vermouth

Serves 1

1. Stir with ice and strain into cocktail glass.

If you know the name of the Prince song inspired cocktail desired, use this index. All cocktails are listed alphabetically in each section.

index

340

Duane Tudahl; Prince and the Parade and Sign O' The Times Era Studio Sessions 1985 and 1986; Published by Rowman & Littlefield Publishers; 2021.

Duane Tudahl; Prince and the Purple Rain Era Studio Sessions 1983 and 1984, Expanded Edition; Published by Rowman & Littlefield Publishers; 2018.

icollector.com; 4155 Prince Graffiti Bridge Script with Handwritten Notes; https://www.icollector.com/Prince-Graffiti-Bridge-Script-with-Handwritten-Notes_i29054540; February 15, 2018.

Kory Grow; Hear Prince's Giddy New Floor-Stomping Track 'Funknroll'; RollingStone; September 19, 2014.

Love4OneAnother; Website; PrinceOnlineMuseum.com; 1999; ? of the Week. [http://princeonlinemuseum.com/love4oneanother/home99.html;]

Marc 'Moose' Moder; Sheena Easton: Looking back at her musical history; Windy City Times; August 8, 2012.

Michael Dale; David Henry Hwang Recalls The Time He Wrote A Song With Prince; Broadway World; April 22, 2016.

NPG Twitter Account / @Prince account (Twitter)—in a response to a fan question by @_dirtydiana97 asking "is there a HitNRun Phase 2 coming out someday?", the response by @Prince3EG was: "Warner Bros. Records WB HAS IT ALREADY. PETITION THEM 2 RELEASE IT." When the same fan asked for any titles of songs included, the account confirmed that Big City was included, followed later by re-posting a 54-second snippet of the track previously shared in October 2013. The tweet that included the link to the Big City snippet read: "WARNER BROTHERS "BIG CITY" SHOUT ... C'MON U'ALL, WE CAN WORK THIS OUT!"

Parents Music Resource Center (PMRC) — was an American committee formed in 1985 with the stated goal of increasing parental control over the access of children to music deemed to have violent, drug-related or sexual themes via labeling albums with Parental Advisory stickers. One of the actions taken by the PMRC was compiling a list of fifteen songs in popular music, at the time, that they found the most objectionable.

This list is known as the "Filthy Fifteen" and consists of the following songs along with the lyrical content category for which each song was considered objectionable:

1. Prince   "Darling Nikki"   Sex/Masturbation
2. Sheena Easton   "Sugar Walls"   Sex
3. Judas Priest   "Eat Me Alive"   Sex/Violence
4. Vanity   "Strap On 'Robbie Baby'"   Sex
5. Mötley Crüe   "Bastard"   Violence/Language
6. AC/DC   "Let Me Put My Love Into You"   Sex
7. Twisted Sister   "We're Not Gonna Take It"   Violence
8. Madonna   "Dress You Up"   Sex
9. W.A.S.P.   "Animal (Fuck Like a Beast)"   Sex/Language/Violence
10. Def Leppard   "High 'n' Dry (Saturday Night)"   Drug and alcohol use
11. Mercyful Fate   "Into the Coven"   Occult
12. Black Sabbath   "Trashed"   Drug and alcohol use
13. Mary Jane Girls "In My House"   Sex
14. Venom   "Possessed"   Occult
15. Cyndi Lauper   "She Bop"   Sex/Masturbation

[https://en.wikipedia.org/wiki/Parents_Music_Resource_Center]

Per Nilsen and jooZt Mattheij with the Uptown staff; The Vault: the definitive guide to the musical world of Prince; Published by Uptown; 2004.

Prince; The Beautiful Ones; Published by Penguin Random House; 2019.

Prince Online Museum; Timeline For Online Archive Of Prince's Official Websites; Prince Online Museum Website; August 9, 2021.

Wikipedia The Free Encyclopedia; Lavaux; Wikipedia Website; March 29, 2021.

Wikipedia The Free Encyclopedia; Lion of Judah; Wikipedia Website; August 2, 2021.

Lee Rudquist

André Akinyele is an American-Canadian author, entrepreneur, and musician.
A Prince fan since the age of 6 (1978), he has attended every Prince show since
the mid-80s and owns every Prince album including rarities on vinyl and CD.
André has recorded under several names including Marcel and Ajamu Akinyele.
He is the founder and leader of the San Francisco bay area jazz/funk/fusion band
Gemini Soul; rock band Looking for Lester (credited as Rebellion); and electronic
duo Lavender Lush (credited as Chambliss Charlie). Based in Toronto, André now
spends much of his time writing books and developing games and software
applications. He draws on an eclectic mix of writing styles, including Prince for
his music projects, as the inspiration for many of his spellbinding projects.

Other Book Titles by André Akinyele include:

Elliptical: The Music of Meshell Ndegeocello

So What's The Big Deal About Scrum? A Methodology Handbook For Developers

Albums by André Akinyele include:

(Does Not Include albums as Marcel, Ajamu Akinyele, or with Gemini Soul, Looking for Lester, Lavender Lush)

Uniqlo Boy

Telegram Mews

The Unauthorized Playlist

Metal Skin and Ivory Birds

The Potomac Syndrome

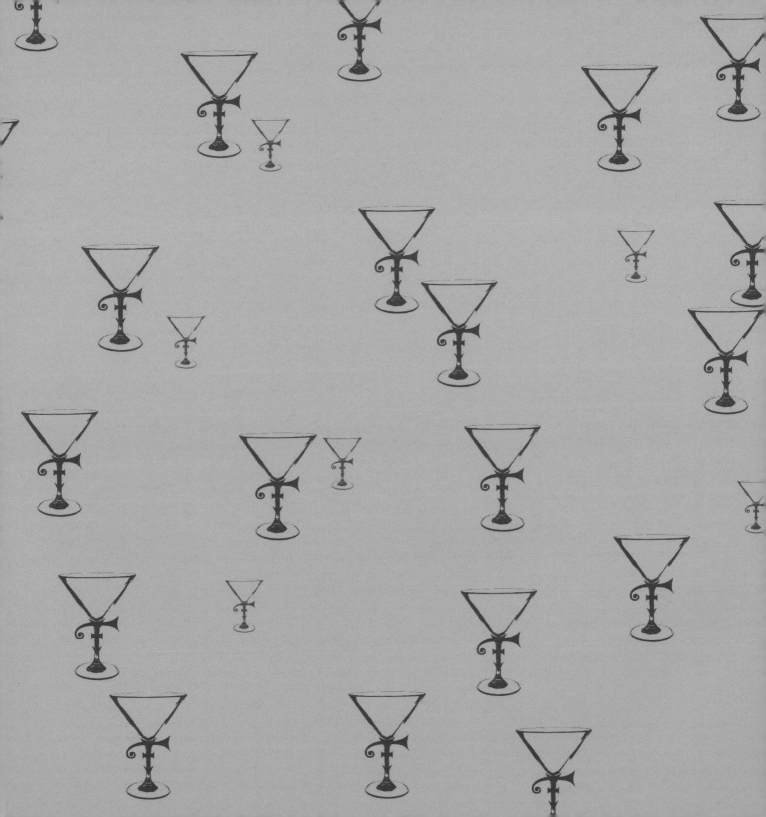

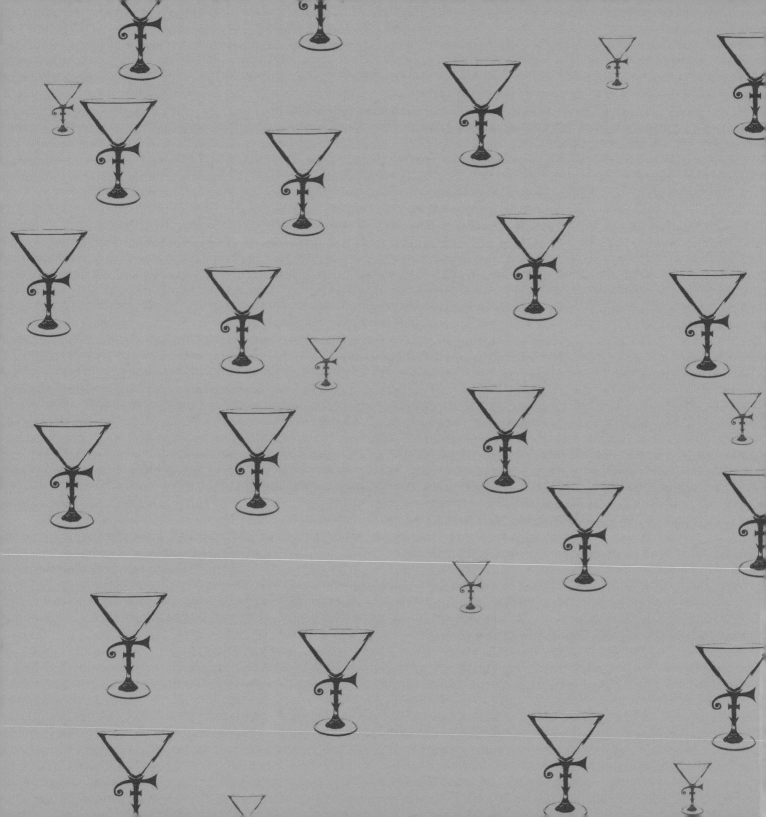